CLIMBING TREE FROGS

by Ruth Berman
photographs by John Netherton

 Lerner Publications Company • Minneapolis

1998

DEC

Website address: www.lernerbooks.com

Curriculum Development Director: Nancy M. Campbell

Words in *italic type* are explained in a glossary
on page 30.

Library of Congress Cataloging-in-Publication Data

Berman, Ruth.
    Climbing tree frogs / by Ruth Berman ;
photographs by John Netherton.
        p.   cm. — (Pull ahead books)
    Includes index.
    Summary: Introduces the physical characteristics,
behavior, and habitats of North American tree frogs.
    ISBN 0-8225-3605-6 (hardcover : alk. paper). —
    ISBN 0-8225-3611-0 (paperback. : alk. paper)
    1. Hylidae—Juvenile literature. [1. Tree frogs.
2. Frogs.] I. Netherton, John, ill. II. Title. III. Series.
QL668.E2B47 1998
597.8'7—dc21   . 98–2679

Manufactured in the United States of America
1 2 3 4 5 6 – JR – 03 02 01 00 99 98

What kind of animal
has a foot like this?

This animal is a tree frog.

Tree frogs are great climbers.

How do you think these frogs climb?

Tree frogs have pads
on the ends of their toes.

These pads are wide and sticky.

The sticky pads help tree frogs
hang on to plants,

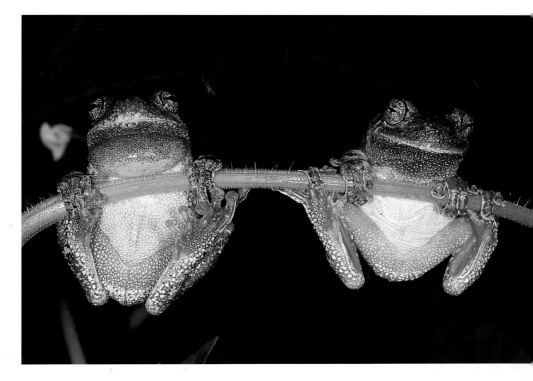

so the frogs can climb
without slipping.

Tree frogs climb to hunt for insects.
Tree frogs are *carnivores.*

Carnivores are animals
that eat other animals.

A tree frog catches insects
with its long, sticky tongue.

A tree frog is a kind of animal called an *amphibian.*

Most amphibians live part of their lives in water.

They live the other part
of their lives on land.

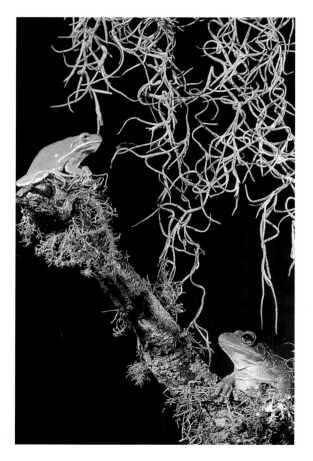

Tree frogs
live mostly
on land,
in trees.

Tree frogs go to the water
to look for partners.

This male frog is calling out
to a female. CRONK!

Male frogs use their *vocal sacs* to call out.

Vocal sacs are bubbles of skin that fill with air.

After the
frogs find
partners,
they lay
eggs in
the water.

The eggs
are soft.
They stick
to plants.

What will
hatch from
the eggs?

Tadpoles hatch from the eggs.
Tadpoles are baby frogs.

At first a tadpole has a tail
and no legs.

It lives underwater. It does not look much like a frog.

Soon the tadpole grows legs.

Then the tadpole leaves
the water.

It looks more like a frog now.

Young adult frogs
are called *froglets.*

This froglet does not have
a tail anymore.

Frogs go through *metamorphosis.*

Metamorphosis is the change
from egg to tadpole to adult.

Adult tree frogs
no longer live in water,

but they still must keep
their skin wet.

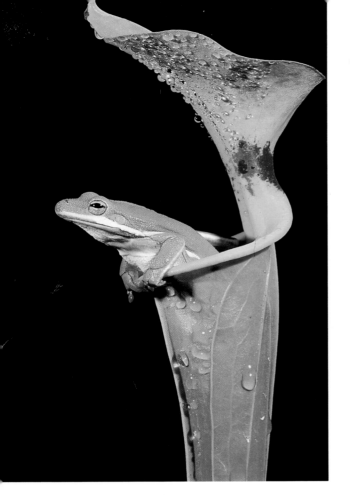

Tree frogs
get water
from rain
and wet air.

They can drink and breathe
through their wet, slimy skin!

The skin of tree frogs can change color. Do you know why?

The skin
changes
color
to help
frogs hide.

The skin also changes color to help frogs cool down or warm up.

Sunshine bounces off light-colored skin, helping a frog cool down.

Sunshine soaks into darker skin,
helping a frog warm up.

Tree frogs are *ectotherms*.

Ectotherms need sunshine
to heat their bodies.

Tree frogs climb and call. They are slimy and sticky and shy.

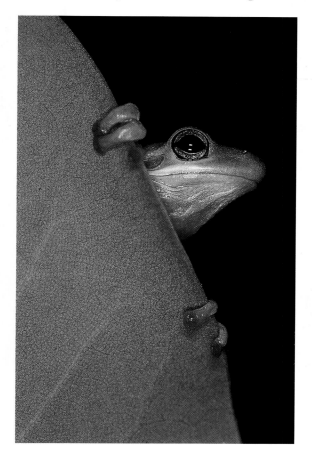

Have you seen a tree frog in your backyard?

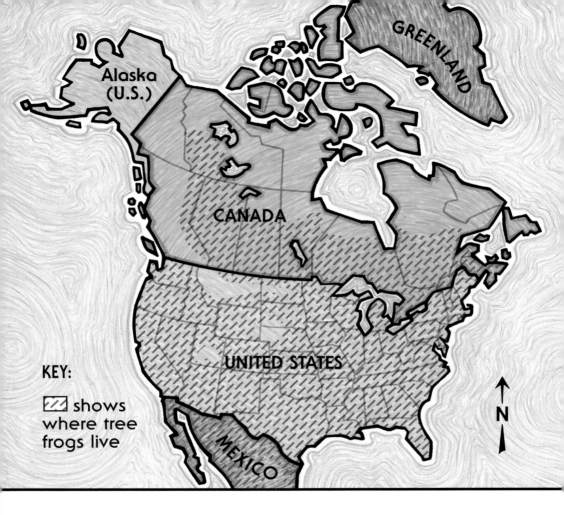

KEY:

▨ shows where tree frogs live

Find your state or province on this map.
Do tree frogs live near you?

Parts of a Tree Frog's Body

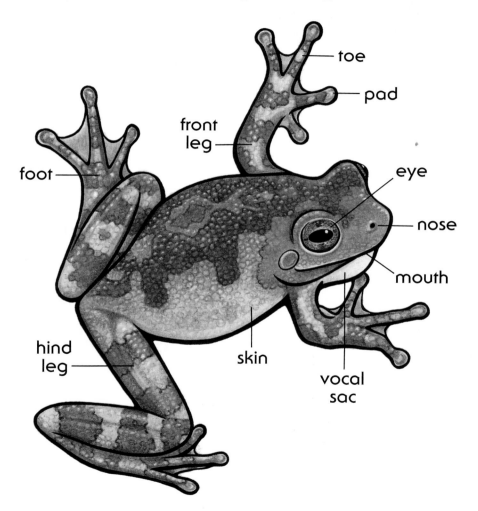

toe

pad

front
leg

foot

eye

nose

mouth

hind
leg

skin

vocal
sac

Glossary

amphibian: an animal that has slimy skin and usually spends part of its life in water and part on land. (Frogs, toads, and salamanders are amphibians.)

carnivores: animals that eat other animals

ectotherms: animals whose body heat changes to match the warmth or cold around them

froglets: young adult frogs

hatch: to come out

metamorphosis: the change in a frog from egg to tadpole to adult

tadpoles: baby frogs

vocal sacs: bubbles of skin that fill with air to help tree frogs call out

Hunt and Find

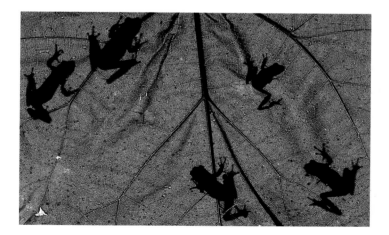

The publisher wishes to extend special thanks to our **series consultant,** Sharyn Fenwick. An elementary science-math specialist, Mrs. Fenwick was the recipient of the National Science Teachers Association 1991 Distinguished Teaching Award. In 1992, representing the state of Minnesota at the elementary level, she received the Presidential Award for Excellence in Math and Science Teaching.

About the Author

Robin Buckley

Ruth Berman was born in New York and grew up in Minnesota. As a child, she spent her time going to school and saving lost and hurt animals. Later, Ruth volunteered at three zoos and got her degree in English. She enjoys writing science books for children. She has written six books in Lerner's Pull Ahead series. Her other books include *Ants, Peacocks,* and *My Pet Dog* (Lerner Publications) and *Sharks* and *American Bison* (Carolrhoda Books). Ruth lives in California with her husband Andy, her dog Hannah, and her two cats Nikki and Toby.

About the Photographer

Brenda Campbell

John Netherton has been a nature photographer for more than thirty years. He has taught and traveled throughout the United States and in many other countries. His work has been published in hundreds of books and magazines. Through these he shares his respect for nature and his commitment to recording it carefully. John has provided photos for four books in Lerner's Pull Ahead series. He lives in Nashville, Tennessee, and is the father of three sons: Jason, Joshua, and Erich.